THE SWORD OF MOSES

AN ANCIENT BOOK OF MAGIC.
FROM AN UNIQUE MANUSCRIPT.

WITH INTRODUCTION, TRANSLATION, AN INDEX
OF MYSTICAL NAMES, AND A FACSIMILE

BY
M. Gaster, Ph.D.

London, 1896

THE SWORD OF MOSES.

I. Introduction.

Magic has exercised the deepest influence upon mankind from remote antiquity unto our own days. It either formed part of the religion of the country, as it was the case in ancient Egypt and Babylon and as it is now in some forms of Buddhism (Tibet), or lived an independent life side by aide with the recognized religion. In some instances it was tolerated, or rendered less obnoxious, by a peculiar subdivision into white or beneficial and black or evil magic, or was downright persecuted. Wherever we go, however, and especially if we turn to the popular beliefs that rule the so-called civilized nations, we shall always and everywhere find a complete system of magical formulas and incantations. The belief in the witch and wizard, and their powerful filters and charms, holds still stronger sway upon human imagination than appears at first sight.

It is remarkable that we do not possess a good work, or exhaustive study, on the history and development of Magic. It is true that we find allusions to it, and sometimes special chapters devoted to the charms and incantations and other superstitious customs prevailing among various nations in books dealing with such nations. But a comprehensive study of Magic is still a pious (or impious) wish. One cannot gainsay that such an undertaking would present extreme difficulties. The material is far too vast, and is scattered over numberless nations and numerous literatures. Besides, much of ancient times has disappeared; in fact, there is a profound gap between antiquity and modern times which is not by any means bridged over by the literature of the Middle Ages. In these times magical art and practice were ruthlessly persecuted by the Church, and the Councils teem with denunciations against the work of the Evil One. Moreover, it was connected in a certain degree with the teachings and practices of the various heretical sects, and the pursuit was anything hut harmless. Thus it comes about that an exhaustive study of the origin and development of Magic is still a wish for the future, and the full influence which it has exercised upon mankind cannot be investigated in such a manner as to have a scientific value until at least a portion of the ancient literature will again have come to light.

The syncretistic character of the Gnostic teachings shows itself also in the adoption of Magic, and in the spiritual interpretation with which they invested the forms and formulas of Magic. The adherents of the various teachings of the Gnostics, and especially those that lived in Egypt and Palestine, adopted all the ideas that were floating about and transferred them into their system of superior Gnosis.

If anything of the teachings of the Gnostics has survived, it is the thaumaturgical portion of it. This has always been popular with the masses, as it afforded them those means which they wanted to defend themselves against the attacks of unseen evil spirits, and to the more speculative minds it afforded a clue to the mystery of the universe. It gave them the means to subdue and to put to their service the unknown forces of nature. This lies at the root of the general acceptance of magic formulas and enchantments, and gives to this practice the popularity which it still retains.

Being the most formidable sects that assumed an anti-Christian character, although some are anterior to Christianity, the Gnostics were the first to be attacked by the Fathers of the Church. Most of the ancient writings of the Fathers are filled with polemics against heretics, of which these are the foremost. The result of this campaign, which lasted for centuries, has been the absolute destruction of all the writings of the Gnostics. Sparse and incoherent fragments only have come down to us, and we are now compelled to study their systems and superstitions, if we may call them so, from the writings of their antagonists, Irenæus and Hippolytus, Tertullian and Epiphanius. A single exception is the work known as "Pistis Sophia," the date of whose composition is variously assigned to the second or fourth century. It certainly seems to belong to a later stage in the development of the Gnosis, as it contains some of the later ideas. It has come down to us in a very bad state of preservation.

Within the last few years the soil of Egypt has rendered some more fragments of this kind of literature, and magic Papyri have now enriched our hitherto very scanty stock of genuine ancient literature. These belong to the second and third century, and, being exclusively of Egyptian origin, throw an unexpected light upon the form which Magic assumed under the influence of the new order of ideas. It is a fact that nothing is so stable and constant than this kind of mystical literature. The very nature of a mystic formula prevents it from ever being radically changed. As there is no other reason for its efficacy than the form in which it is pretended to have been fixed or revealed to the Select by the Divinity itself, any change of *that* form would immediately destroy its efficacy. Dread preserved the form intact, at least as long as the practitioner stood under the influence of those divinities whose power he invoked for protection, or as long as he believed in the power of those demons whose malignant influence he tried to avert by means of that form of enchantment. This explains the uniformity of a number of such charms in whatever language we find them and almost to whatever time they may belong; as long as they are the outcome of one and the same set of religious ideas, which is the determining factor. But with the change of religion the charms also undergo changes, not in the *form* but in the names of the divinities invoked, and these bring other changes with them. To take a modern example, the charm against the Evil Eye will contain the name of Christ or of a Saint in a Christian charm, the name of Muhammad in the Muhammedan, and that of an angel or a mysterious name of God in the Jewish formula, though all the rest would be identical. The same process happened also in ancient times, and the Papyri mentioned above assist us in tracing the change which the new order of ideas had introduced in the magical formulas of the Christian era.

If we trace the first impulse of these changes to the Gnostics, we must at once associate it with the sects of Essenes and Theraupeuts that swarmed in Egypt and Palestine, and with the most important sect of Gnostics which produced the greatest impression, i.e. that represented by Valentin. His is the one against whom most of the polemics of the Fathers of the Church were directed. He is the author of the most profound and luxuriant, as well as the most influential and the best known, of the Gnostic systems. He was probably of Egyptian-Jewish descent ; and he derived his material from his own fertile imagination, from Oriental and Greek speculations, and from Christian ideas. In his system entered also the mystical combinations of letters and signs known under the name of cabalistic formulas, and he moreover favored the permutations and combinations of letters to express divine names and attributes. To him we owe the theory of Æons and the Syzygies, or divine creative pairs, of which the two first form together the sacred "Tetraktys." I believe this to be the Gnostic counterpart of the sacred "Tetragrammaton," and not, as has hitherto been assumed by others, the Tetraktys of the Pythagoreans. For one can see in his system, and more so in the mystical part of it, the direct influence of the Jewish mystical speculations of the time. Valentin lived, moreover, in Palestine, and nothing would suit him better than to manipulate that mystical, Ineffable Name of God, round which a whole system had been evolved in the service of the Temple. Angelology and mysterious names of God and His angels are, moreover, intimately connected with the above-mentioned sects.

The mysterious Ineffable Name of the divinity which is invoked seems to be the center of moat of the ancient and even modern Magic. By knowing that Name, which is assumed to be the name by means of which the world was created, the man or exorciser in Egypt pretended to constrain the god to obey his wishes and to give effect to his invocation if called by his true name; whilst in Chaldea the mysterious Name was considered a real and divine being, who had a personal existence, and therefore exclusive power over the other gods of a less elevated rank, over nature, and the world of spirits. In Egyptian magic, even if the exercisers did not understand the language from which the Name was borrowed, they considered it necessary to retain it in its primitive form, as another word would not have the same virtue. The author of the treatise on the Egyptian mysteries attributed to Jamblichus maintains that the barbarous names taken from the dialects of Egypt. and Assyria have a mysterious and ineffable virtue on account of the great antiquity of these languages. The use of such unintelligible words can be traced in Egypt to a very great antiquity.

It is necessary to point out these things in order to understand the character of the new formulas which take now the place of the old. To the old and in time utterly unintelligible names, new names were either added or substituted, and the common source of many of these names is Jewish, mystical speculation. The Ineffable Name of God and the fear of pronouncing it can be traced to a comparatively remote antiquity. We find in those ancient writings that have retained the traditions of the centuries before the common era, the idea of a form of the Ineffable Name composed of 22, 42, or 72 parts, or words, or letters, of which that consisting of 72 was the most sacred. It is still doubtful what those 22, 42, and 72 were -- either different *words* expressing the various attributes of God, or *letters* in a mystical combination; but whatever these may have been they took the place of the Ineffable mystical name and were credited with the selfsame astounding powers. By means of these every miracle could be done and everything could be achieved. All the powers of nature, nil the spirits and demons could be subdued, and in fact there was no barrier to human aspiration. The heavens were moreover peopled at a very early age with numberless angels arranged in a hierarchical order and each endowed with a special Name, the knowledge of which was no less desirable for working miracles. I need only allude to Dionysius Areopagita to have mentioned a complete treatise of such a divine economy recognized by the Church, but we can go much higher up and find these divisions and subdivisions of the celestial hosts recorded in books that belong to the second era before Christ. In the *Book of Enoch* (ch. vi) we have a long list of such names of angels, and in a book, the date of which has been differently put, the names of angels are still more numerous, to which there are added also various names of God. The book in question pretends to be a vision of the high Priest Ismael, and is a description of the heavenly halls. Modern scholars who knew nothing of the Gnostic and other heretic literature put it as late as the ninth century, simply and solely because they could not find early traces of it in the old literature, and because it seemed to appear first in those times. A comparison of it with the Ascensio Iesaiae, and still more with a chapter in the "Pistis Sophia," easily convinces us, however, of the fact that absolutely similar treatises were known as early as the first centuries after Christ, if they were not, in fact, later remakings of still more ancient texts. The Greek Papyri already alluded to have also this peculiarity in common with these texts, that they abound in similar lists of names of angels and demons borrowed from Egyptian, Christian, and Jewish sources. Among these we find also numerous forms of the Name of God consisting also of a number of letters, 7, 27, and others, and also most curious combinations of letters.

The Jewish idea of a mystical Name of God rests thus upon the interpretation of the Tetragrammaton, or the word JHVH, that stands for God in the Hebrew text, which from very ancient times the priests first and then the whole people refrained from pronouncing in the way it was written. A substitute was found for it, so as to avoid a possible profanation of the sacred Name. But it is an object of millenary speculation what that substitute really was. As already remarked, it is represented by a changing number of elements, letters or words. The original miraculous, powerful Name, however, was the Tetragrammaton known as the "Shem ha-meforash." This word has presented great difficulties to the following generations. It can be translated either as meaning *explicit*, the "explicit" Name of God, whilst the others are merely substitutes, or *separate*, the name which is used exclusively for the designation of the Divinity. These two are the best known and most widely accepted interpretations of the "Shem ha-meforash." In the light, however, of our study it will appear that another translation will henceforth be found to be the only true one, at any rate for ancient times. Later on the true meaning of this expression was lost, and one or the other of the first-mentioned philological translations was adopted. So we find in the *Testament of Solomon, e.g.,* "the angel called Aphoph, which is interpreted as Rafael." Considering that this name was believed to be the only True Name of God, the all-powerful name which was never pronounced, "Shem ha-meforash" can only mean the Ineffable, as we find it also in the "Pistis Sophia," and all throughout the ancient tradition. It is an euphemism; instead of saying: it is the "Ineffable" unutterable name, they used the word which meant: it is the "explicit" name, just as they said for a "blind" man -- he is "full of light"; other examples can be easily adduced. In this way an ancient mystery and a stumbling-block for the translator of such texts disappears.

As the Tetragrammaton, or "Shem ha-meforash," was the Ineffable Name, and could by no means ever be uttered, others were substituted and were used by the priest when blessing the people. These also were endowed with a special sanctity, and were revealed only to the initiated. These substitutes were considered to be no less effective for miracles, and the knowledge of these mysterious Names was no less desirable than that of the true Tetragrammaton, for they were believed to represent the exact pronunciation of the forbidden word, and thus to contain part, if not the whole, of the power with which the Tetragrammaton itself was invested. Rab, a scholar who had studied in Palestine towards the end of the second century, says of these substituted names, and more especially of that of forty-two elements (Tr. Kiddushin, fol. 71a) : "That this Name is to be revealed only to a man who stands in the middle of his life, who is pious and modest, who never gives way to anger and to drink, who is not obstinate. Whoever knows that Name and preserves it in purity is beloved in heaven and beloved upon earth; is well considered by man and inherits both worlds." What these forty-two may have been has thus far been the object of speculation. When comparing the ancient tradition with the new texts in the Papyri, and in the mystical texts of Hebrew literature, there can no longer be any doubt that the Name of forty-two, or more or less, elements could not have been originally anything else but *words* consisting of that *number of letters*, which were substituted in the public pronunciation for the Ineffable Name consisting of one word and only *word* and only *four letters* -- the Tetragrammaton! In time these substitutes were also forgotten, or not divulged, and thus arose a series of new substitutes and variations for the divine Name. There was also the fear of profaning the name of God when writing it down in the way it occurred in the Bible, and therefore they resorted to manifold devices on the one hand to avoid a possible profanation, and on the other to obtain sacred or mysterious substitutes for the Ineffable Name.

Another element that came within the purview of this activity of coining new names was the new and greatly developed angelology that flourished at that time in Palestine and Egypt. The angels had to be provided with appropriate and powerful names, and the authors resorted to the same devices, of which I mention the most prominent, and which are the cause of many of the barbarous forms and names that abound in the magical rites and formulas and in the so-called practical Cabbalah. The biblical names of Michael, Gabriel, and others with the termination -el = God served as a model for some of the new angels, such as in the *Book of Enoch* and in other similar writings. The first part was, as a rule, taken from the characteristic attribute connected with the activity of that new angel: so *Raphael* = the healing angel, in the *Book of Tobit*; *Raziel* = the angel of the mysteries; and in the same manner a boat of similar names. Then came into requisition the system of permutation of the letters of the divine name: one standing first was placed at the end, and so on. Much more extensively were the change in the order or the substitution of other letters resorted to. In the Alphabet of R. Akiba no less than five different systems of this kind of substitutions are enumerated; either the last letter of the alphabet stands for the first (A-t; b-sh, א״ת ב׳ ש׳ etc.), or one letter stands for the one immediately preceding such, as b for a; or the eighth and fifteenth stand for the first, and so on (A-h-s; b-t'-a, אחס בטע), or first and twelfth are interchangeable (A-l; b-m, א׳ל ב׳מ). One can easily see how differently the same name could be written and employed in the same amulet, and all these various forms representing only *one* and the same name. The Tetragrammaton appears, therefore, either as מצפץ, or כוזו, or כקרק, or שעפש etc. The number of such permutations and substitutions is not limited, however, to these four systems enumerated; they are innumerable, and it is almost impossible to find the key for all met with in these mystical writings, and especially on the amulets.

Other means employed for the purpose of devising new variations and protections for the sacred name, belonging to the very eldest times, were the combination of *two* words into *one*, of which one is a sacred name and the other an attribute, but the letters of these two words are intermingled in such a manner that it is not always easy to decipher them. An example, which has hitherto not been understood, we have already in the Talmud. The High Priest Ismael is said to have seen Iah אכתריאל *Aktriel* in the Temple. This word, which stands for the mysterious name of God, is nothing else than the combination of the two words כתר *Ktr* = Crown and *Ariel*, from Isaiah xxix, 1. In the text, which I publish here, we have the name שקרחזי *Skdhzi* = שרי and חזק *Hzk* = mighty, powerful. Names were further formed by leaving out one or two letters from the Tetragrammaton or from ether sacred names of the Bible, the primary reason always being to avoid the possibility of profanation, as the profane utterance of the divine name brought heavy penalty upon the culprit. In this manner is the obscure exclamation in the Temple to be understood, אני והו *Ani vhu*, instead of the usual "O Lord" (help us) : in each of these two words one letter has been left out -- the *d* in the first, *Adni*, and the second *h* in the second word. On other occasions strange letters were inserted between those of the divine name, and thus we get the puzzling form (Tr. Synhedrin, 56a = vii, 5) which is mentioned when the blasphemer who had blasphemed God was brought before the judges. The judges ask the witnesses to repeat the blasphemy uttered by the accused, and they say,

instead of mentioning the Divine Name, the words
יְכה יֹוסהֹאת יוסי, which may have obtained this form in
our printed texts through popular etymology, meaning "Jose
beat Jose!" But originally we have here clearly the
Tetragrammaton יְהֹוה, and a strange letter inserted after
each letter of that word, viz. כ, י, ס, . and א

This process continues still unto our very days, but from the
thirteenth or fourteenth century onwards a change has taken
place in the system of the formation of these mysterious
words, considered to be so efficacious in amulets. The initials
of the words of a biblical verse are combined into a new word
without any meaning, or the letters of a verse are so arranged
as to form uniform words of three letters without meaning,
the commencement of each of these words being the letters of
the Hebrew words arranged consecutively. The most
celebrated example is the use to which Exodus xiv, 19-21 has
been put for many a century. But these are a mark of more
recent origin, and not a trace is to be found throughout the
whole ancient mystical literature, and also not in our text.

If we should apply these principles to the Greek Papyri, there
is no doubt that a key might be found for the innumerable
curious names which crowd these fragments of a literature
that at one time must have been very rich. Traces of it we find
also in the "Pistis Sophia," where special stress is laid upon
that Ineffable Name, communicated only to the initiated.
The knowledge which a man acquires through the "Nomen
Ineffabile" is described at some length (pp. 131-153). In
another place we read that Jesus spoke the Great Name over
the disciples whilst preaching to them, and blew afterwards
into their eyes, by which they were made to see a great light

(p. 233). The mysterious names of God and of the Powers are enumerated on pp.223 and 234-5, whilst the following passage explains the power of that Name:-- "There is no greater mystery than this. It leads your soul to the light of lights, to the places of truth and goodness, to the region of the most holy, to the place where there is neither man nor woman nor any definite shape, but a constant and inexpressible light. Nothing higher exists than these mysteries after which ye seek. These are the mysteries of the seven voices, and their forty-nine Powers, and their numbers, and no name is superior to that Name in which all the other names are contained, and all the Lights, and all the Powers. If anyone knows that Name when he goes out of the material body, neither smoke nor darkness, neither Archon, angel, or archangel, would be able to hurt the soul which knows that Name. And if it be spoken by anyone going out from the world and said to the fire, it will be extinguished; and to the darkness, and it will disappear; and if it be said to the demons and to the satellites of the external darkness, to its Archons, and to its lords and powers, they will all perish, and their flame will burn them so that they exclaim 'Thou art holy, Thou art holy, the Holy of all the Holy.' And if that Name is said to the judges of the wicked, and to their lords and all their powers, and to Barbelo and the invisible God, and to the three Gods of triple power, as soon as that Name is uttered in those regions they will fall one upon the other, so that being destroyed they perish and exclaim ' Light of all the Lights, who art in the infinite lights, have mercy upon us and purify us.'" This is almost identical with the saying of Rab, with the difference that in the "Pistis Sophia" the Egyptian influence is not yet wholly obliterated. These examples suffice to show the character of the central point in the new Magic adopted by the Gnostics, viz. , the mysterious Divine Name and its substitutes derived from the mystical speculations of Palestine, and also the general tendency of syncretism and absorption of various forms and invocations in that form of Magic which henceforth will have the deepest influence upon the imagination and belief of the nations of the West.

From that period, then, up to the twelfth or thirteenth century there is a gap which neither Psellus nor the Testament of Solomon fill sufficiently. All those ancient magical books, being declared the work of the evil spirit, were successfully hunted up and destroyed. The link which binds the literature of the second half of the Middle Ages with the past is missing, and we find ourselves often face to face with the problem whether a book that appears after that period is of recent origin, or is an ancient book more or less modified? Such a book is, for instance, the so-called Sefer Raziel, or the book delivered to Adam by the angel Raziel shortly after he had left Paradise. It is of a composite character, but there is no criterion for the age of the component parts. The result of this uncertainty is that it has been ascribed to R. Eleazar, of Worms, who lived about the middle of the thirteenth century. One cannot, however, say which portion is due to his own ingenuity and which may be due to ancient texts utilized by him. I am speaking more particularly of this book as it seems to be the primary source for many a magical or, as it is called now, a cabbalistical book of the Middle Ages. Trithemius, the author of "Faust's Hoellenzwang," Agrippa, and many more, are deeply indebted to this book for many of their invocations and conjurations, although they must have had besides similar books at their disposal, probably also the Clavicula Solomonis, the Great Grimoire, etc.

I must still mention one more fragmentary relic of that literature, viz. the inscribed cups and bowls from ancient Babylon with Aramaic inscriptions. These belong partly to the Lecanomantia, and are another example of the constancy of these formulas; for centuries these remain almost unchanged, and even in their latest form have retained a good number of elements from the ancient prototype.

It so happened, then, that some inquisitive men living in Kairouan, in the north of Africa, should address a letter to the then head of the great school in Babylon, Haya Gaon (d. 1037), asking him for information on various topics connected with magic rites and the miraculous powers ascribed to the Ineffable Name. I give here the gist of some of their questions, which date therefore from the second half of the tenth or the commencement of the eleventh century. They ask first, what it is about that Ineffable Name and other similar mysterious Names of angels through the means of which people can make themselves invisible, or tie the hand of robbers, as they had heard from pious men from Palestine and Byzantium that if written upon leaves of reeds (Papyri!) or of olive trees and thrown in the face of robbers would produce that effect; and if written on a potsherd and thrown into the sea, calms it; or placed upon a corpse, quickens it to life; and, further, that it shortens the way so that man can travel immense distances in no time. They have also books with these terrible, awe-inspiring Names, and with the *seals* of those celestial powers of which they are terrified; as they know that the use of these mysterious Names, without due and careful preparation, brings with it calamity and premature death. To these and other questions the Gaon gives a sensible and philosophic reply, warning them, in the first instance, not to place too much credence on the statements of people who pretend to have seen, but to try and see with their own eyes. Then he goes on to tell them that such books with mystical names are also to he found in his college, and that one of his predecessors was known to have been addicted to these studies, and to the writing of amulets and the knowledge of incantations, but, he adds, "only a fool believes everything." As for the books with formulas, he goes on to say: "We have a number of them, such as the book called 'Sefer ha-Yashar,' and the book called '*The Sword of Moses*,' which commences with the words, 'Four' angels are appointed to the Sword,' and there are in it exalted and miraculous things; there is, further, the book called 'The Great Mystery,' besides the minor treatises, which are innumerable. And many have labored in vain to find out the truth of these things." In the course of his reply Haya touches also upon the Ineffable Name and the name of seventy-two (elements), which, according to him, was the result of the combination of three biblical verses (*cf.* above, p. 11, where reference is made to Exodus xiv, 19-21), but he neither knows which they are nor how they were uttered; as to the other of forty-two, he says that it consisted of forty-two *letters*, the pronunciation of which was, however, doubtful, resting merely upon tradition. This name commenced, according to him, with the letters אבגיתץ *Abgits*, and finished with שקוצית *Skusit*. He mentions further the books-- "The Great and the Small Heavenly Halls" and "The Lord of the Law," full of such terrifying names and *seals* which have had that dreaded effect upon the uncalled, and from the use of which those before them had shrunk, lest they be punished for incautious use.

These abstracts suffice to show that the mystical literature had not come to an end with the third or fourth century, but had continued to grow and to exercise its influence throughout the whole intervening period. The reasons why so little is mentioned in the contemporary literature is, that each period has its own predilections, Subjects which absorb almost exclusively the general interest, and are therefore prominently represented by the literature of the time, whilst other things, though in existence, are relegated to an obscure place. The best example we have is the modern folklore literature, that has assumed such large proportions, no one pretending that the subject did not exist throughout the centuries, although neglected by scholars. It must also not be forgotten that we have only *fragments* of the literature that flourished in Palestine and among the Jews in the Byzantine empire, to which countries this mystical literature belongs. Christian literature leaves us also in the dark for this period, for the reasons stated above; only Syriac might assist us somehow to fill up that gap, but as far as I am aware very little is to be expected from that quarter, as in the whole magnificent collection of the British Museum I have not found a single MS. of charms or magical recipes, except one single, rather modern, Mandaic text. Two very small, and also rather modern, Syriac MSS. of charms are in the possession of the Rev. H. Gollancz.

Of those books now mentioned by Uaya Gaon in his reply -- all of which, by the way, seem to have been irretrievably lost -- I have had the good fortune to discover one, viz. that called "*The Sword of Moses*," of which he gives us the first words. From the answer of Haya it is evident that he considered this book to be old and to be the most important, for he is not satisfied with merely giving the title as he does with the other books, but he makes an exception for this to indicate the commencement and to add that it contained "exalted and wonderful things." A glance at the contents of the newly-discovered text will justify the judgment of Haya, for it is a complete encyclopedia of mystical names, of eschatological teachings, and of magical recipes.

Before stating the contents I must first give a short description of this MS., now Cod. Hebr., Gaster, 178. This text has come to me with a mass of other leaves full of magical formulas, all in a very bad state of preservation and apparently hopelessly mixed up. Happily there were custodes at the ends of the leaves, and by their means I was enabled, after a long toil and careful handling of leaves falling to pieces on account of old age and decayed through dampness to recover a good portion of the original MS. and the whole of this text, which occupies twelve small quarto leaves. The number of lines varies. The writing belongs to the thirteenth or fourteenth century, and is in Syrian Rabbinical characters. It is evidently a copy from a more ancient text, and the copyist has not been very careful in the transcript he made. Many a letter is written wrongly, having been mistaken for another similar, such as ד (D) for ר (R) and ם (M) for ס (S). In many a place there are evident lacunae, and the copyist has often not understood the text. The language is a mixture of Hebrew and Aramaic, Hebrew prevailing in the first part, which I call the Introductory or historical, as it gives the explanation of the heavenly origin of this text, and deals with all the preliminary incidents connected with the mode of using the text in a proper and efficacious manner. In the last, which I call the theurgical or magical part, Aramaic prevails. All the diseases are mentioned in the language of the *vulgus*, and so also all the plants and herbs, and the other directions are also in the same language. To no language, if I may say so, belongs the middle part, which is the real text of the "Sword." This consists of a number of divine and mysterious Names, a good number of which are the outcome of all those modes of manipulations with the letters briefly indicated above. It would be a hopeless task to try and decipher these names, and to transliterate them into the original forms of which they are the transformations and mystical equivalents. In this section we can recognize besides the unchangeable character of some of the magic formulas. What I said before of the Egyptians, who would not change any sacred Name, however barbarous it may sound, for fear of destroying its efficacy, holds good also for another number of Names found here in a bewildering variety. Almost every religion must have contributed to the list that makes up the "Sword." Eclecticism would be a mild word for this process of general absorption, that has made the "Sword" thus far the most complete text of magical mysterious Names which has come down to us. A small encyclopedia of a similar character is the Greek Papyrus of the British Museum, No. cxxi, and the Leyden Papyrus (J. 395), with which our text shows great similarity, but these Papyri mark as it were the first stages of this process of growth by the assimilation of various elements and combination into one single complete *vade-mecum* for the magician or conjurer. In the "Sword" we have the full development of that process, which must have run its course at a very early period.

Nothing is more fallacious than to try etymologies of proper names. The omission or addition of one letter by a careless copyist suffices to lead us completely astray. It is, therefore, difficult to advance any interpretation of even a few of the names found in this text that have a familiar appearance. If we were sure of the reading, we might recognize among those in No. 6, Isis (Apraxia, Veronica), Osiris, Abraxas, and others;

but, as already remarked, such an identification might easily lead us astray, and the coincidences might only be the result of mere chance. No doubt can, however, be entertained as to the complex character of this text, and to the astounding form of many of the names which it contains. It is a systematically arranged collection ; in the apparent disorder there is order ; and the names are placed according to certain leading features which they have in common. Thus we have a long string of names that are composed with the word Sabaoth (Nos. 24-37); others that are the components of the divine -*el* (Nos. 102-34). More startling still is a list of supposed names of heavenly powers that are represented as *sons if* of other powers. These are undoubtedly derived from many sources, the author welding smaller texts and lists into one comprehensive list. The third part contains the directions for the application of these various Names. These are also arranged according to a certain system. The diseases follow, at any rate in the first portion, the order of the members in the human body, commencing with the head and its parts, then descending to the lower members; after which follow recipes for ailments of a different nature, to be followed by the directions for performing miracles and other remarkable feats.

Each of these 136 items (numbered by me) corresponds with a certain portion of Part II, the words or the mystical Names of those portions in Part II being the mysterious words that alone were the proper to have the expected magical result. In order to facilitate research, I have subdivided Part II into such corresponding portions to which I give the same number. There is thus an absolute parallelism between the two parts-one the text and the other its magical application. We see that the book has been very methodically arranged by one who intended to prepare as complete a magical book as possible.

By this parallelism, and by the partial repetition of the mysterious words in Part III, we have the means to satisfy ourselves as to the accuracy of the copyist, who does not come out very satisfactorily from this test. It may be that the original from which he copied was already partly corrupt, and the fear which such books inspired prevented him from attempting to correct what are obvious mistakes in the spelling of those Names. It not seldom happens that the same Name is written in two or three different forms in one and the same recipe. I have also not attempted any correction, as we have no means to decide which of these *variæ lectiones* is the true and which the corrupt. Another reason why the copyist may be exonerated from at least some of these inconsistencies, is the fact that he gives in many places what are intended to be different readings. lie starts his copy with the marginal note, unfortunately half gone, the paper being destroyed in that place, that "there are differences of opinion as to the readings of the text and of the Names," or, as I would interpret this mutilated glosse, "the marginal readings are *variæ lectiones*." For, in fact, there are a good number of marginal glosses throughout Parts I and II.

There also are some in Part III, but these are of a totally different character. They are purely philological, and furnish one powerful proof more both for the antiquity of the text with which we are dealing and for the country where the MS. has been copied. Most, if not all, these glosses are, namely, *Arabic* translations of the Aramaic words of the original. By the mistakes that have crept into these Arabic glosses, it is evident that they have not been added by the copyist, who surely would have known how to write his own translation, but who would make mistakes when copying another MS., especially if it were in any way badly written or had suffered in consequence of age. The translation further proves that the original was written at a time when Aramaic was the language of the people, and that at a certain time when the copy was made from which this MS. is a transcript the language of the original had begun to be forgotten and required a translation, which, by the way, is not always exact. The Aramaic of this text is, in fact, not easy to understand; there occur in it many words of plants and diseases which I have not found in any dictionary in existence, and many of the grammatical forms present peculiar dialectical variations, which point to Palestine as the original home of our text, and deserve a special study. Here again we have to lament the fact that we deal with an unique manuscript and have no means to test the accuracy of the text. But even as it is, this text will prove an extremely valuable contribution to Semitic philology, and would enrich even Löw's book on Aramaic names of plants, where I have in vain searched for the names and words occurring in our text. I have therefore added a translation, which, however, in some places, does not pretend to be more than an attempt to grapple with a very recalcitrant text.

The title of the book seems to be derived from the last words spoken by Moses before his death. He concludes his blessing of the Children of Israel with these words (Deuter. xxxiii, 29): "Who is like unto thee, a people saved by the Lord, the shield of thy help, and that is the Sword of thy excellency," or "thy excellent Sword." The figurative "Sword" spoken of here must have been taken at a later time to signify more than a figure of speech. Under the influence of the mystical interpretation of Scripture flourishing at a very early period, it was taken to denote a peculiar form of the divine Name, excellent and all-powerful, which served as a shield and protection. It therefore could be made to serve this purpose in magical incantations, which did not appeal to tile assistance of demons but to the heavenly hosts obeying the command of the Master of that "Sword." There is no wonder, then, that it came to be connected with the name of Moses, the very man who spoke of it, and whose last words were of that "Sword." In the Greek Papyri, Moses is mentioned as one who keeps divine mysteries (Brit. Mus., Pap. xlvi, of the fourth century, lines 109 ff., ed. Kenyon, in Catalogue, 1893, p. 68, and note to it) ; and again, in another Papyrus, cxxi, of the third century (*ibid.* p. 104, l. 619 and note), a reference to one of tile magical books ascribed to Moses, called "The Crown of Moses." But what is more important still, the Leyden Papyrus calls itself the eighth Book of Moses. It resembles very much our text, which has thus preserved the old name by which many of these magical books went. Dieterich, who published the Leyden Papyrus (Abraxas, Leipzig, 1891), looks to Orphic origins for that magical composition and lays too great stress on the Cosmogony in it. In the light of our text it will become evident that these go all back to one common source, viz. to the mystical speculations of those sects, which lie himself enumerates (pp.136 ff.) ; and the "Logos ebraikos" quoted by him from the Paris Papyrus (*ibid.* pp. 138-141) shows more clearly still the same sources for all these compositions. The overwhelming importance assigned in these texts to the "holy Name" consisting of a number of *letters*, and the book calling itself "The Work of Moses on the Holy Name," justify us in seeing in it an exact parallel to the Hebrew text, recovered now by me. There is much internal similarity between the Hebrew "Sword" and the Greek Papyri. The order of subjects is similar; all commence with an eschatological part, which in the Greek is more in the nature of a Cosmogony, in the Hebrew that of the description of the heavenly hierarchy. In both follows the "Name," and after that a list of magical recipes which refer back to that Name. The constant refrain of the Leyden Papyrus after each recipe is: "Say the Name! " Here the Name is still simple; in the Hebrew text it is represented by the rich variety which I have pointed out, but an intimate connection between these various texts cannot be doubted.

There exists besides another small treatise (B), also unique, that goes under the same name as "The Sword of Moses" (Cod. Oxford, 1531, 6). It is a short fragment of a different recension, and has only a remote resemblance with the first text (A). It consists of a list of mystic Names, different in their form from the other text, and has only sixteen recipes, which do not correspond with *portions* only of the first part, but, as in the Leyden Papyrus, the whole of this was to be repeated after each recipe. Immediately upon this short text follows an invocation of the heavenly Chiefs, attributed to Ismael, the High Priest, the reputed author of the "Heavenly Halls." This addition corresponds to a certain extent with the first part of the "Sword" (A). In none, but very few exceptions, of B is there any trace of Aramaic, and a totally different spirit pervades the whole text. It is in the first place doubtful whether we have here the whole of it or merely a fragment. In two places we find the letters גנ (NG) and גד (ND), which taken as numerals mean 53 and 54. If they stand for such, then we have here only the last two or three portions of a long text, of which the preceding 52 are missing. Again, on the other hand, as it is regularly recommended to repeat the whole of the "Name" after each recipe, an operation that would be well-nigh impossible for the inordinate length of that text, those NG and ND may not stand as numbers of paragraphs. This text presents besides many more peculiar traits that make it rather remarkable. We find here thus far the only trace in Hebrew literature of the "Twins" or Didymoi" which appear in the Gnostic hymns of the apocryphal Acts of the Apostle Thomas, and are brought into connection with the system of Bardesanes, The heavenly Powers mentioned in the "Sword" (A) under the form of *sons* of other Powers, point also to the same system of Bardesanes, of whom Ephraem Syrus said: "He invented male and female beings, gods and their children." He may have taken these ideas from older sources. However it may be, this coincidence is none the less remarkable. We find further angels with double names, the one of which I translated "Kunya," *i.e.* the proper name, and the other the *explicit*, i.e. *Ineffable* unutterable name, corresponding entirely with that of the Testament of Solomon, where we find "the angel called Apharoph interpreted Raphael"

(τῷ καλουμένῳ Ἀφαρώφ, ὅ ἑρμηνεύεται ʹΡαφαὴλ. -- Orient, 1844, col. 747).

In the Gnostic prayer from the Acts of the Apostle Thomas, the Sophia is spoken of as the one "who knows the mysteries of the Chosen," or, according to the Syriac version, "revealer of the mysteries of the Chosen among the Prophets." With this the passage in the Hebrew text (B) may be compared, where the same idea is enunciated; and one feels almost tempted to see in the inexplicable word קיִין ("Kinn") the Greek "Koinôn," the companion or partaker of the mystery; although it seems rather strange to find the very word in the Hebrew text. But there are many words that have a peculiar appearance in this text, and they look like transliterations of Greek words in Hebrew characters, such as "Chartis

27

Hieratikon," etc. I have added, therefore, this second text also, making thus the publication of the "Sword" as complete as possible.

As a second Appendix I have added two conjurations found in the MS. of the "Sword " (A), both in Aramaic, and extremely interesting also for their similarity with the inscriptions inside the bowls brought from Assyria and Babylon. A detailed study of some of these magic bowls and their inscriptions has been published by M. Schwab.

I have reproduced all these texts as closely and accurately as possible, without attempting any corrections or emendations, except in the case of obvious mistakes, which are pointed out by me as corrections. The glosses are given as notes, and the few corrections of obvious mistakes. I have refrained from referring to inscriptions on Gnostic gems and amulets, where we find "Ephesia grammata" similar to those of Part II of the "Sword" (A) and to some of Appendix I, and to the magical formulas in the terra-cotta bowls, which present a striking similarity with some portions of "The Sword." One cannot exhaust a subject of this kind, and the utmost one can attempt to do is to place as ample a material as possible at the disposal of those who make the study of Magic and theurgy and of the so-called practical Cabbalah the object of special enquiry. I have limited myself to draw attention to the relation that exists between these, the Greek Papyri, and the Hebrew texts which I publish here for the first time, and to point out the important fact that we have now at least one fixed date from which to start in the enquiry of a subject in which dates and times have thus far been very doubtful. It is, moreover, a contribution to Semitic philology, and by the addition of a facsimile of the first page a contribution to Semitic palæography.

The origin of the "Sword" is none the less somewhat difficult to fix. From the letter of Haya Gaon it is evident that it must have been at least a few centuries older than his time (tenth century). But it must be much older still. As the Leyden Papyrus belongs at the latest to the third century, and those of the British Museum to the third or fourth century, we are justified in assigning to the first four centuries of the Christian era the origin of our Hebrew text, which throws so vivid a light upon those remnants of Greek Magic buried hitherto in the soil of Egypt. Herein lies also one side of the importance of our text, that it shows how the connection between antiquity and the later ages was maintained. The Greek texts had become inaccessible and practically lost to the world, whilst the Hebrew text, written in a language which was considered sacred, the knowledge of which was never allowed to be extinguished, preserved the ancient magical texts, with their curious mystical names and formulas, and carried them across the centuries, keeping up the old tradition, and affording us now a glimpse into a peculiar state of the popular mind of those remarkable times. The careful study of those Greek fragments side by side with the Hebrew will assist very materially in the understanding also of those often very obscure texts, and lift the study from the narrow groove in which it has hitherto been kept by the classical scholars who have devoted their attention recently to them. It will also help us in laying bare the fountains from which flowed the whole of the magical arts of the Middle Ages.

II. TRANSLATION
The Sword of Moses.

In the name of the mighty and holy God!

Four angels are appointed to the "Sword" given by the Lord, the Master of mysteries, and they are appointed to the Law, and they see with penetration the mysteries from above and below; and these are their names -- SKD HUZI, MRGIOIAL, VHDRZIOLO, TOTRISI. And over these are five others, holy and mighty, who meditate on the mysteries of God in the world for seven hours every day, and they are appointed to thousands of thousands, and to myriads of thousands of Chariots, ready to do the will of their Creator, , the Lord of Lords and the honoured God; these are their names -- X . And the Master of each Chariot upon which they are appointed wonders and says: "Is there any number of his armies?" And the least of these Chariots is lord and master over those (above) four. And over these are three chiefs of the hosts of the Lord, who make every day tremble and shake His eight halls, and they have the power over every creature. Under them stand a double number of Chariots, and the least of them is lord and master over all the above Chiefs (rulers); and these are their names -- X . And the name of the Lord and king is X , who sits, and all the heavenly hosts kneel, and prostrate themselves before Him daily before leaving X , who is the Lord over all.

And when thou conjure him he will attach himself to thee, and cause the other five Chiefs and their Chariots, and the lords that stand under them, to attach themselves to thee just as they were ordered to attach themselves to Moses, son of Amram, and to attach to him all the lords that stand under them; and they will not tarry in their obeisance, and will not withhold from giving authority to the man who utters the conjuration over this "Sword," its mysteries and hidden powers, its glory and might, and they will not refuse to do it, as it is the command of God X saying: "Ye shall not refuse to obey a mortal who conjures you, nor should you be different to him from what you were to Moses, son of Amram, when you were commanded to do so, for he is conjuring you with My Ineffable names, and you render honour to My name and not to him. If you should refuse I will burn you, for you have not honoured Me."

Each of these angels had communicated to him (Moses) a propitious thing for the proper time. These things (words) are all words of the living God and King of the Universe, and they said to him: --

"If thou wishest to use this 'Sword' and to transmit it to the following generations, (then know) that the man who decides to use it must first free himself three days previously from accidental pollution and from everything unclean, eat and dring once every evening, and must eat the bread from a pure man or wash his hands first in salt (?), and drink only water; and no one is to know that he intends using this 'Sword,' as therein are the mysteries of the Universe, and they are practised only in secret, and are not communicated but to the chaste and pure. On the first day when you retire from (the world) bathe once and no more, and pray three times daily, and after each prayer recite the following Blessing: --

"Blessed art thou , O Lord our God, King of the Universe, who openest the gates of the East and cleavest the windows of the firmament of the Orient, and givest light to the whole world and its inhabitants, with the multitude of His mercies, with His mysteries and secrets, and teachest Thy people Israel Thy secrets and mysteries, and hast revealed unto them the "Sword" used by the world; and Thou sayest unto them: "If anyone is desirous of using this 'Sword,' by which every wish is fulfilled and every secret revealed, and every miracle, marvel, and prodigy are performed, then speak to Me in the following manner, read before Me this and that, and conjure in such and such a wise, and I will instantly be prevailed upon and be well disposed towards you, and I will give you authority over this Sword, by which to fulfil all that you desire, and the Chiefs will be prevailed upon by you, and my holy ones will be well disposed towards you and they will fulfil instantly your wishes, and will deliver to you my secrets and reveal to you my mysteries, and my words they will teach you and my wonders they will manifest to you, and they will listen and serve you as a pupil his master, and your eyes will be illuminated and your heart will see and behold all that is hidden, and your size will be increased." Unto Thee I call, X , Lord of the Universe. Thou art He who is called X , King of the Universe. Thou art called X , merciful king. Thou art called X , gracious king. Thou art called X living king. Thou art called X , humble king. Thou art called X , righteous king. Thou art called X , lofty king. Thou art called X , perfect king. Thou art called X , upright king. Thou art called X , glorious king. Thou art called X , youthful king. Thou art called X , pleasant king. Thou art called X , and thou listenest to my prayer, for Thou hearkenest unto prayer; and attach unto me Thy servants the lords of the "Sword," for Thou art their king, and fulfil my desire, for evening is in Thy hands, as it is written: "Thou openest thine hand and satisfiest every living being with favour."

"I conjure you, Azliel called X ; I conjure you, Arel called X , Ta'aniel called X , Tafel called X , and the most glorious of these Yofiel Mittron called X , the glory from above. With the permission of my king (I conjure) Yadiel called X , Ra'asiel called X , Haniel called X , Haniel called X , Asrael called X , Yisriel called X , A'shael called X , Amuhael called X , and Asrael called

X , that you attach yourselves to me and surrender the "Sword" to me, so that I may use it according to my desire, and that I find shelter under the shadow of our Lord in heaven in the glorious Name, the mighty and awe-inspiring X , the twenty-four letters from the Crown; that you deliver unto me with this "Sword" the secrets from above and below, the mysteries from above and below, and my wish be fulfilled and my word. hearkened unto, and my prayer (supplication) received through the conjuration with the Ineffable name of God which is glorified in the world, through which all the heavenly hosts are tied and bound; and this is the Ineffable Name -- X , blessed be he! (I conjure you) that you shall not refuse me nor hurt me, nor frighten and alarm me, in the tremendous Name of your king, the terror of whom rests upon you, and who is called X . Fulfil for me everything that I have been conjuring you for, and serve me, for I have conjured you not with the name of one who is great among you but with that of the Lord over all, whose name ties and binds and keeps and fastens all the heavenly hosts. And if you should refuse me, I will hand you over to the Lord God and to his Ineffable name, whose wrath and anger and fire are kindled, who honours his creatures with one letter of his name, and is called X ; so that if you refuse he will destroy you, and you will not he found when searched after. And you preserve me from shortness of spirit and weakness of body in the name of X , the guardian of Israel. Blessed art Thou, who understandest the secrets and revealest the mysteries, and art king of the Universe.'"

A voice warn heard in the heavens, the voice of the Lord of heavens, saying: "I want a light (swift) messenger (to go) to man, and if he fulfils my message my sons will become proud of the 'Sword' which I hand over to them, which is the head of all the mysteries of which also my seers have spoken, that thus will my word be, as it is said: 'Is not my word like as fire? saith the Lord'"

(Jer. xxiii, 29). Thus spoke X , the lord of heaven and earth; and I, Assi Asisih and Apragsih , the light (swift) messenger, who am pleased with my messages and delighted with my sending, ascended before Him, and the Lord over all commanded me: "Go and make this known to men who are pious and good and pure and righteous and faithful, whose heart is not divided and in whose mouth is no duplicity, who do not lie with their tongues and do not deceive with their lips, who do not grasp with their hands and are not lustful with their eyes, who do net run after evil, keep aloof from every uncleanness, depart from every defilement, keep themselves holy from contamination, and do not approach woman." When the Lord ever all commanded me thus, I, X , the swift messenger, went down to earth, and I said on my way: "Where is the man who possesses all these that I should go to him and place this with him?" And I asked myself, and thought in my heart that there is no man who would do all this that I wished; and I found none, and it was heavy unto me. And the Lord over all conjured me by His mighty right arm, and by the lustre of His glory and His glorious crown, with an oath of His mighty right arm, and He conjured me, and the lord over all strengthened me and I did not fall. I thus stood up, I, X , to put NN in the possession of the desired covenant, in the name of X ."

"This is the great and glorious Name which has been given as a tradition to man -- X , holy, glorious, glorious, Selah. Recite it after thy prayers. -- And these are the names of the angels that minister to the son of man -- Mittron, Sgrdtsih, Mqttro, Sngotiqtel, etc., etc., etc. (28 names) ." "In a similar manner shall you serve me NN; and receive my prayer and my orisons, and bring them to God X , blessed be He! for I adjure you in His name, and I extol you (to ascend), like unto the bird that flies from its nest, and remember my meritorious deeds before Him and (make Him) forgive now my sins on account of my words of supplication, and you may not refuse me in the name of X , blessed be He! Sabaoth, Sabaoth , Selah. His servants sanctify Him and praise Him with sweet melody, and say: "Holy, holy, holy is the Lord of holy name; the whole earth is full of His glory"; and do not refuse me, in the name of X, who lives for ever, and in the name of Ditimon, etc., X, and in the name X of the great One from whom nothing is hidden, who sees and is not seen, and in the name of Him who is the chief over the heavens and is called X. And the King of the Universe utters (this name) also in a different manner, thus -- X. You swift messenger, do not tarry and do not frighten me, but come and do all my wants in the name of X, the great One, who sees and is not seen, AHVH, whose Ineffable Name is revealed to the heavenly hosts; and I conjure you by this Ineffable Name, such as it was revealed to Moses by the mouth of the Lord over all, X, the Lord Sabaoth is His name. Blessed art thou, O God, lord of mighty acts, who knowest all the mysteries."

And which are the letters which X communicated to Moses? He said to him: "If thou wishest to get wise and to use the 'Sword,' call me, and conjure me, and strengthen me, and fortify me, and say: 'X, with the great, holy, wonderful, pure, precious, glorious, and awe-inspiring secret Name X, with these letters I conjure thee to surrender to me and make me wise and attach to me the angels which minister to the "Sword," in the name of the Revealer of mysteries. Amen.'"

Write with ink on leather and carry about with you during those three days of purification, and invoke before and after prayer the following Names communicated to Moses by Mrgiiel, X, by Trotrosi, X, etc. (the 13 Chiefs mentioned at the beginning, and a long string of other mysterious names which are said to have been communicated to Moses). "And they have not hidden from him any of these sacred Ineffable names or letters, and have not given him instead the Substitutes of any of these sacred letters, for thus were they ordered by the Lord of all mysteries to communicate to him this 'Sword,' with these Names which constitute the mysteries of this 'Sword'; and they said to him 'Command the generations which will come after thee to say the following blessing prior to their prayer, lest they be swept away by the fire': 'Blessed art Thou, X , who wast with Moses; he also with me, Thou, whose name is X. Send me X, who is the cover of the Cherubim, to help me. Blessed art Thou, Lord of the Sword.'"

Whoever is desirous of using this 'Sword' must recite his usual prayers, and at the passage "Thou hearkenest to prayer" say: "I conjure you four princes X, servants of Hadirion, X, that you receive my invocation before I pray, and my supplication before I entreat, and fulfil all my wishes through this 'Sword,' as you have done to Moses, in the glorious and wonderful name of the Lord of wonders, which is interpreted thus -- X." He must then call the five superior Chiefs and say: "I conjure you, X, that you accept my conjuration as soon as I conjure you, and you attach to me those four princes and all the hosts of Chariots over which you preside, to fulfil all my wishes through this 'Sword' by this beloved name X." He must then call the three angels that are superior to these, and say: "I conjure you, X, the beloved of X, who is Hadiririon, that you attach yourselves to me and attach to me X, who are standing under your rule, to fulfil all my wishes through this 'Sword' by this unique name X." And then he must lay hold of the highest Chief over all and say: "I conjure thee, X, strong and powerful Chief over all the heavenly hosts, that thou attachest thyself to me, thou and not thy messenger, and attach to me all the Chiefs that are with thee, to fulfil my wishes through this 'Sword,' by the name X, which has no substitute, for thou art beloved and he is beloved, and

I am from the seed of Abraham called the beloved. Blessed art thou, King of the mysteries, Lord of the secrets, who hearkenest unto prayer."

And he is not to touch this "Sword" ere he has done all these things; afterwards he will be able to do whatever he likes, everything being written here following in its proper order.

II. This is the "Sword."

: "With these your Names, and with the powers you possess, to which there is nowhere anything like (I conjure you) to show me and to search for me, and to bring me X to do all my bidding in the name of X," and, again, a list of names, that have no special characteristic in common. Nos. 20-24 are all names commencing with JJ; some of these finish with JH. 24-36 all these names have the word Sabaoth attached to them. To 41-47 HVH is added. From Nos. 51-93 all the names are composite; they appear as names of sons, the name of the father being added to each of these, close upon 160 names, e.g.: Sagnis, son of Srngia; Ssgn, son of 'Arggis; Atumi, son of Batumi; Ahsuti, son of Kkthus; Agupi, son of Abkmi, etc. Every name from 102 on to the end of this part finishes with -el, after which follow varying syllables and words: some are only JH or JV (Nos. 102-105), or a word commencing with 'A- and finishing with -JH (Nos. l06-lll). Nos. 112-121 are followed by ARVH, whilst 122-l27=JHVHH, and Nos. 128-134=HVJH. They conclude with the following words: "Ye sacred angels, princes of the hosts of X, who stand upon the thrones prepared for them before Him to watch over and to minister to the 'Sword,' to fulfil by it all the wants by the name of the Master over all; you Chiefs of all the angels in the world, X, in the name of X the seal of heaven and earth, ministers of X the most high God; through you I see X in the world; you are lording over me in all the place of the Master over all: I pray of you to do everything that I

38

am asking of you, as you have the power to do everything in heaven and upon earth in the\ name of X, as it is written in the Law, 'I am the Lord, this is My name!'"

III.

1. If at full moon (?) a man wishes to unite a woman with a man that they should be as one to one another, to destroy winds (spirits), demons, and satans, and to stop a ship, and to free a man from prison, and for every other thing, write on a red bowl from Tobar, etc. (No. 1). -- 2. To break mountains and hills, to pass dryshod through the water, to enter the fire, to appoint and to depose kings, to blind the eyes, to stop the mouth, and to speak to the dead, and to kill the living, to bring down and to send up and to conjure angels to hearken unto thee, and to see all the mysteries of the world, write Nos. 1 and 2 upon the saucer of a cup and put in it the root of genip-tree (genipa). -- 3. Against a spirit that moves in the body write on a plate No. 3. -- 4. Against a spirit that burns write No. 4. -- 5. Against a spirit in the whole body write No. 5-6. Against a demon (shidda) write No. 6. -- 7. Against shingles write No. 7. -- 8. Against quinsy (erysipelas?) say the words of No. 8 over oil of roses and put it over his face. -- 9. For pains in the ear whisper in the painful ear No. 9. -- 10. For aches in the eye say the words No. 10 over water three days running in the morning, and wash the eye with it. -- 11. For cataract say the words of No. 11 over oil of sesame, and anoint the eye with it during seven mornings. -- 12. For grit in the eye say over Kohl No. 12, and fill the eye with it for three mornings. -- 13. For blood that runs from the head whisper No. 13 over the head early in the morning for three days, when you wash your hands before getting out of bed. -- 14. For paralysis say seven times over a vessel full of water and seven times over sesame-oil the words No. 14, "that it should move away and leave NN, Amen, Amen, Selah"; and throw the pail of

water over his head and anoint him with the oil, and do this for three days; then write an amulet with the words from, "I conjure you " till "Amen, Selah," and hang it round his neck. -- 15. For pains in one half of the head (neuralgia?) and for bad singing in the ear, write No. 15 and hang it round the neck. -- 16. For the bad deafening (of the ear) write No. 16 and hang it round the neck. -- 17. For pains in the ear say into the left ear the words No. 17 backwards. -- 18. For deafness say over hemp water, whilst mixing it with oil of "Idi" (sesame?), the words of No. 18, and put it into his ear as soon as it has become a little dissolved (or warm). -- 19. For scabs, ulcers, itches, mange, shingles, etc., that befall mankind, say over olive oil No. 19 and anoint with the left hand. -- 20. For jaundice say the words No. 20 over water in which radish has been soaked, and let him drink it. -- 21. For pains in the nose and for the spirit in the nose say No. 21 over oil of "Idi" (sesame?) and put it into his nostrils. -- 22. For pains in the stomach (lit. heart) and in the bowels say No. 22 over water, and drink it. -- 23. For hot fever say No. 23 over water in which rose-laurels are soaked, and he is to bathe in it. -- 24. For tumors, etc., say No. 24 once over them and once over olive oil, and anoint them for three days, but do not let any water come near them -- 25. For an evil occurrence (?) say No. 25 over seven white cups of water, filled from the river, and throw them over the head. -- 26. For ulcer (diphtheria?) spit out before him, and say over his mouth, and over a cup of strong drink, No. 26, and make him drink, and watch what is coming out of his mouth. -- 27. For a man bitten by a snake or by another (!) poisonous insect, he must say over the place of the bite or over the painful spot No. 27 and drink it; the same he is to do whenever hurt by any creeping thing. -- 28. For a woman who has seen blood before the time my No. 28 over an ostrich egg, then burn it, and she be smoked with it. -- 29. For pains in the mouth say No. 29

over risen flour, and put it upon his mouth. -- 30. For quinsy (croup) and for pains in the shoulder, say No. 30 over wine and drink. -- 31. For a painful nerve write No. 31 on a scroll and speak these words over olive oil, and rub some of it on the scroll and smear it over the painful spot and hang the amulet round his neck. -- 32. For stone my over a cup of wine No. 32, and drink it. -- 33. For hemorrhoids take tow and put salt on it and mix it with oil, saying over it No. 33, and sit on it. -- 34. For a man who suffers from swelling and from venereal disease (?), he is to say No. 34 over water in which radishes are soaked, and drink. -- 35. For sprains, either you take a plate and write upon it No. 35 and put it upon the place, and all around it will be healed; or you take a ball of wool and dip it in oil of (sesame?), and say those words upon it and put it upon the sprain. -- 36. When injured or hurt by iron, and for every blow that it should not fester, say No. 36 over white naphtha and rub it over the place of the blow. -- 37. For (cramps?) and for pains of heart say over spinach and oil No. 37, and drink it. -- 38. For the gall and the bowels take the water in which raisins have been soaked, saying over it No. 38, and drink it. -- 39. For the spoiled liver take (a drink) a sixth measure of water-lentils and say No. 39, and swallow it slowly (?). -- 40. For the milt say No. 40 over wine-lees and drink it, and repeat it for three days. -- 41. For the spirit who rests on the womb, say No. 41 on camphor oil and put it on it with a ball of wool. -- 42. For a woman who has a miscarriage, say No. 42 on a cup of wine, or strong drink, or water, and let her drink it for seven days; and even if she should see blood and she repeats it over a cup of wine, the child will live. -- 43. For a man who is bald, say No. 43 over nut-oil and anoint with it. -- 44. To conjure a spirit write on a laurel-leaf: "I conjure thee, prince whose name is Abraksas, in the name of (No. 44) that thou comest to me and revealest to me all that I ask of thee, and thou shalt not tarry." And the one bound by thee will come down and reveal himself to thee. -- 45. To remove a rich man from his riches, say No. 45 upon the dust of an ant-hill and throw it into his face. -- 46. To heal leprosy, take the patient to the side of the river and say to him: "I conjure thee, leprosy, in the name of (No. 46) to disappear and to vanish, and to pass away from NN. Amen, Amen, Selah"; and he is to go down and dip seven times in the river, and when he comes out write an amulet with the words "I conjure -- Selah," and hang it round his neck. -- 17. For diarrhea write No. 47 on a red copper plate and hang it round his neck.

-- 48. If thou wishest that the rain should not fall upon thy garden, write out No. 48. -- 49. If thou wishest to see the sun (!) take . . . from a male tree and stand in front of the sun and say . . . which art called on the . . called . . . and the ears of barley (?) the words of No. 49;2 and he will appear unto thee in the form of a man dressed in white and he will answer thee upon everything that thou askest him, and he will even bring a woman after thee. -- 50. Whosoever wishes to enter a furnace is to write No. 50 on a silver plate and hang it upon his haunch.

-- 51. If thou seest a king or a ruler and thou wishest that he follow thee, take a basin of water and put into it the root of genip-tree, and the root of purslane, and the root of (Artilochia), and say No. 51, and place it on fiery coals in a white earthen vessel and throw upon them leaves of olive-tree, and whatever thou decreest he will bring unto thee, even a woman thou canst command. -- 52. If you wish to overawe them, take water from the fountain and say upon it No. 52 and throw it into their faces. -- 53. For loosening (any charm) say over water No. 53 and throw it over him and write it as an amulet and hang it round his neck, and also for freeing a man from prison. -- 54. To catch fish, take a white potsherd, and putting into it leaves of olive-tree say over them No. 54 at the side of the river. -- 55. If thou wisheat a woman to follow thee, take thy blood and write her name upon a newly-laid egg and say towards her No. 55.--56. If a man is to follow thee, take a new potsherd and dip it in black myrrh (gall) and pronounce over his name the words of No. 56, and walk on without looking backwards. -- 57. For a tree that does not produce fruits, write the words No. 57 upon a new potsherd and bury it under the root of the fruitless tree, and water all the trees and these also which do not produce the fruit. -- 58. For illness (dog) in the fruit write on a new potsherd No. 58 and bury it in the cistern (watering-place), and say these words also over water, ashes, and salt, and water the earth with it. -- 59. For a suckling babe write on an onyx slab No. 59 and whisper it into its ears three times, spitting out after the whispering; then repeat them over a cupful of water 70 times and give it the child to drink. -- 60. For one bitten by a rabid dog, write No. 60 on the halter of an ass and let the ass go; then repeat these words over sesame oil and let him anoint himself with it and put on new clothes and hang that halter (?) round him. -- 61. For fever and small fever, write on the skin of the brains of a ram or a goat No. 61, and hang it round his neck. -- 62. If anyone lose his way he is to say No. 62 over the four corners of his belt (?). -- 63. If thou wishest to ask anything of thy neighbour, say No. 63 over oil of sesame or of . . . or of . . . -- 64. If thou wishest that a woman is to follow thee write thy name and her name with thy blood upon her door, and the same upon thy door, and repeat the words of No. 64.-65. If thou wishest to know whether thy journey will be lucky, take a field lettuce with open leaves, and standing before the sun say the words of No. 65 and watch the lettuce: if the leaves close and shut, then do Dot go; but if they remain in their natural state, proceed, and thou wilt prosper. -- 66. If thou wishest to deliver a man from prison (?) say No. 66 once to him, and once to the sun, and once to the prison (?) house. -- 67. To conquer (collect?), take dust from thy house and say over it seven times in the road of the town the words of No. 67, and then take dust from the road and do likewise and throw it into thy house. -- 68. If you wish to kill a man, take mud from the two sides of the river and form it into the shape of a figure, and write upon it the name of the person, and take seven branches from seven strong palm-tree. and make a bow from reed (?) with the string of horse-sinew, and place the image in a hollow, and stretch the bow and shoot with it, and at each branch (shot) say the word. of No. 68; and may NN be destroyed . . . -- 69. To send plagues, take (parings?) from seven men and put them into a new potsherd, and go out to the cemetery and say there No. 69, and bury it in a place that is not trodden by horses, and afterwards take the dust from this potsherd and blow it into his face or upon the lintel of his house. -- 70. To send dreams to your neighbours, write No. 70 upon a plate of silver and place it in the mouth (?) of a cock and kill it when it has gone down its mouth, and take it out from the mouth and put it between its legs and bury it at the end of a wall, and put thy foot upon that spot and say thus: "In the name of X, a swift messenger is to go and torment NN in his dreams until he will fulfil my wish." -- 71. If a snake follows thee say No. 71, and it will dry up. -- 72. To stop a boat in the sea, say No. 72 over a potsherd or on a rounded flintstone and throw it against it into the sea. -- 73. To loosen it (from the charm), say No. 73 over dust or a clod of earth and throw it into the water, and as this dissolves the boat gets free to go. -- 74. If thou wishest to prevent an oven or furnace or pot from becoming destroyed (unclean?), say No. 74 over dust and throw it over them. -- 75. If thou wishest them to be hot, spit in front of them and say No. 75, and they will boil. -- 76. If thou wishest to pass dryshod through the sea, say upon the four corners of the head-dress (turban) No. 76, and take one corner in thy hand and the other is (?) to precede thee. -- 77. If thou wishest to curse anyone, say in the 'Eighteen benedictions' No. 77, in the name of X. -- 78. To speak with the dead, whisper No. 71 into his left ear and throw into their holes (?). -- 79. To kill a lion, bear, an adder, or any other hurtful animal, take the dust from under the right foot, say over it No. 79, and throw it into their faces. -- 80. To catch them, take the dust from under your left foot, saying No. 80, and throw it into their faces. -- 81. To open a door, take the root of lotos reed and place it under the tongue and say No. 81 against the door. -- 82. To kill an ox or another beast, say into its ear No. 82-83. To inflame his heart, say No. 83 over a piece of raw meat, and give it to him to eat. -- 84. To make a fool of one, say No. 84 over an egg and place it in his hands. -- 85. To destroy the house of thy neighbour, say No. 85 over a new potaherd and throw it into his house. -- 86. To expose (?) your neighbour, say No. 86 over oil of . . . and smear it at the bottom of his jug (?). -- 87. To make your neighbour disliked, take blood from phlebotomy, say upon it No. 87, and throw it upon his lintel. -- 88. To make a woman have a miscarriage, say No. 88 over a cup of water and throw it over her lintel. -- 89. To make a man ill, say No. 89 over olive ol and let him anoint himself with it. -- 90. To know whether a man a sick person will die or live, say before him No. 90: if he turns his face towards you he will live; if away, he will die. -- 91. To catch a lion by the ear, say No. 91 and make seven knots in the fringes of thy girdle and repeat these words with each knot, and you will catch him. -- 92. To make thy renown go throughout the world, write No. 92 as an amulet and bury it in thy house. -- 93. To shorten the way, say No. 93 over a single lotos reed. -- 94. To cure hemorrhoids, take kernels of dates . . . and burn them in fire and say No. 94, and mix it with oil of olives and place it as an amulet over it, and it will be good. -- 95. For every spirit write upon a bowl No. 95 and hang it round the neck. -- 9b. For subtle poison, as cumin-seed and calamint, write No. 96 upon an egg and put it into wine, and repeat over it the same words and then drink it. -- 97. For the thunder that comes from heaven, take a ring (round piece) of iron and lead, and hang it on the spot you wish (to protect), and say over it No. 97.-98. To go before king or lord, say No. 98 over a piece of lion's skin dipped in black hemp (?) and pure wine, and take it with thee. -- 99. For blight, if it happen, take a sinew and soak it in turnip-juice in the night from Wednesday to Thursday, and say No. 99 over it; on the morrow sprinkle that water over the field. -- l00. If the fruit gets worm-eaten, take a worm from the mud and put it into a tube and say No. 100 over it; then close the tube and bury it in that place. -- l01. To free a man from prison (? shame), say over the grounds of Kappa (?) and unripe dates No. 101, and give it to him to eat. -- 102. For a field that does not produce fruits, take eight cups from eight houses and fill them with water from eight rivers, and put salt into them from eight houses, and say over them No. 102 eight times, and pour out two cups at each corner, and break them on eight paths. -- 103. If one does not know what a man is ailing from, soak mullein (verbascum) in water, and say over it No. 103, and let him drink it when he is thirsty. -- 104. To make war, take the dust from under the left foot, say over it No. 104, and throw it into the (enemies') face, and there will appear knights with weapons in their hands who will fight for thee. -- 105. To throw thy fear upon mankind, write No. 105 upon a leaden plate and bury it on the west side of the Synagogue. -- 106. To have always light in the darkness, write No. 106 upon a chart (paper) and carry it always with thee. -- 107. To catch (blind) the eye, write No. 107 upon a scroll and expose it in a wicker-basket to the stars, but you must not speak when

46

writing. -- 108. To send a sword which should fight for thee, say No. 108 over a new knife wholly of iron, and throw it into their face. -- 109. If thou wishest that they kill one another, say No. 109 over a new knife wholly of iron and bury it with your heel into the earth, and keep the heel upon it in the earth, and they will kilt one another, until you take it out from the earth. -- 110. To make them pause, take the dust from under the right foot, and, saying the same word. again backwards, throw it into their face, and they will stop. -- 111. If an enemy has got hold of thee and wishes to kill thee, bend the little finger of the left hsnd and say No. 111, and he will run away from thee like one who runs away from his murderer. -- 112. To catch the eye (blind), say No. 112 over the skin of a lion and carry it with thee, and no one will be able to see thee. -- 113. If thou fallest into a (?) and wishest to come out, say No. 113, and thou wilt come out in peace. -- 114. If thou fallest into a deep pit, say in thy fall No. 114, and nothing will hurt thee. -- 115. When thou fallest into a deep river say No. 115, and thou wilt come out in peace. -- 116. If any burden or weight falls upon thee, say No. 116, and thou wilt be saved. -- 117. If the king's servants lay hold on thee, bend the little finger of the left hand and say No. 117 before king or judge, and he will kill these people who have laid hands on thee. -- 118. If a host has surrounded thee, turn thy face towards the west and say No. 118 before king or judge, and they will be like unto stones and will not move. -- 119. If thou wishest to release them, turn thy face towards the east and repeat these words backwards. -- 120. If thou walkest in vales or on the mountains and hast no water to drink, lift thine eyes to Heaven and say No. 120, and a fountain of water will he opened unto thee. -- 121. If thou hungerest, lift thine eyes to Heaven and spread out thine arms and say No. 121, and a spirit will stand before thee and bring thee bind and meat. -- 122. If thou wishest to call the angel (prince) of man, say over thy mantle (?) No. 122, and the angel bound by thee will come to thee and will tell thea whatever thou wishest (to know). -- 123. If thou wishest to let him go (depart), say before him the same words backward, and he will depart. -- 124. If thou wishest that any heavenly prince is to come to thee and teach thee, say No. 124 and conjure him in the third hour of the night from: "in the name of the Lord over the holy ones (No. 136) to the and of the 'Sword,'" and "Send him to me that he reveal unto me and teach me all that is in his power," and he will then disappear (!). -- 125. To walk upon the water without wetting the feet, take a leaden plate and write upon it No. 125 and place it in thy girdle, and then you can walk. -- 126. To become wise, remember for three months running, from the new moon of Nissan onwards, the words of No. 126, and add in the 'Eighteen benedictions': "May the gates of wisdom be opened to me so that I should meditate in them." -- 127. To remember immediately all thou learnest, write on a new-laid egg No. 127, then wash it off with strong wine early in the morning and drink it, and do not eat anything for three hours. -- 128. To make another forget what he has learned, write No. 128 in his name on laurel-leaves and bury them under his lintel. -- 129. To send an evil spirit against thy neighbour, take a green grasshopper and say over it No. 129, and bury it in an earth-hill and jump over it. -- 130. To send a plague, take the bone of a dead man and dust from under him in a pot and tie it up in a woven rag with saliva, and say upon it No. 130 in his name, and bury it in the cemetery. -- 131. To tie and to fasten thiefs and robbers, say No. 131, and whilst saying it put your little finger in the ear. -- 132. To release them, say No. 132, and take thy finger out of the ear. -- 133. To guard thy house from thieves, say No. 133 over a cup of water and pour it out round thy roof. Thus also to guard a house. -- 134. To guard a house from hosts (robbers), take earth from an ant-hill and strew it round the roof, repeating the words of No. 134.-135. To guard thyself from Mazikim, say: "In the name of 'Nos. 1-5' may I, NN, pass in peace and not in hurt." The same must be done to excommunicate them when you meet them. -- 136. For every other thing that has not been mentioned say, No. 136 to the end of the "Sword."

And upon every amulet that you write from this "Sword" write first: "In the name of the Lord of all the holy ones, may this 'Sword' be effectual to do my services, and may the lord of it approach to serve me, and may all these powers be delivered over to me so that I be able to use them, as they were delivered to Moses, the son of Amram, perfect from his God and no harm befalling him!" If he will not act accordingly the angels of wrath, ire, fury, and rage will come near him to minister to him, and they will lord over him, and strangle him, and plague him all over. And these are the names of their leaders: the leader of the angels of wrath is Mzpopiasaiel; the name of the leader of the angels of ire is Zkzoromtiel; the name of the leader of the angels of fury is Kso'ppghiel; the name of the leader of the angels of rage is N'mosnikttiel. And the angels that stand under them are numberless, and these all will have power over him, and will make his body like unto a dunghill.

May the Lord preserve you from every evil. Amen!

End of the "Sword," with the assistance of God feared in the council of the holy ones. End, end.

APPENDIX I.

In the name of the Lord. The Sword of Moses.

I. and the angel over the animals, whose name is Ittalainma; and the angel over the wild beasts, Mtnisl; and the angel over the wild fowls and over the creeping things, Trgiaob; and the angel over the deep waters and over the mountains, Rampel; and the angel over the trees, Maktiel; and the angel over the sweet-smelling herbs, Arias; and the angel over the garden fruit, (vegetables), Sofiel; and the angel over the rivers, Trsiel; and the angel over the winds, Mbriel; and over man, X. -- . . . . hours are proper for man to pray aad to ask for mercy upon man, be it for good or evil; and it is said that every hour is proper for man to pray, but during the three first hours in the morning man is to pray and to mention the hundred sacred names and the mighty ones, whose sum amounts to three hundred and four. Amen. Selah!

.... X give me healing ....

Which is the great light? All the . . . . X, I conjure you, mother of the (whether?) male and mother of the (or?) female, you, the "Twins," I conjure you, the hard (strong) spirits, in the name of God, the mighty hero, the living one , in the name of God , . . Raphael (save) me from the Lions, the powerful ones (Archon?), and the Twins. I conjure you, strong spirits, in the name of God, the mighty hero, IH, IHVH, IHVH, I, N, son of N..

II. Verily, this is the ("Sword of Moses") with which he accomplished his miracles and mighty deeds, and destroyed all kind of witchcraft; it had been revealed to Moses in the bush, when the great and glorious Name was delivered to him. Take care of it and it will take care of thee. If thou approachest fire, it will not burn thee, and it will preserve thee from every evil in the world. -- 1. If thou wishest to try it take a thick (green) branch and utter this

"Sword" over it five times at sunrise, and it will dry up. -- 2. To catch fish, take sand from the sea and the root of the date (tree) (or the kernel of the date), and repeat this "Sword" over them, and the fish will come to the spot where thou throwest the sand. -- 3. To walk on the waters of the sea take the wooden helve of an axe, bore a hole through it, pass a red thread through it, and tie it on to thy heel, then repeat the words of the "Sword," and then you may go in and out in peace. -- 4. To run quickly (?), write the "Sword" on "Chartis hieratikon," then put water into a new earthenware pot, and let them drink it and wash their faces, and they will he victorious! -- 5. To break it (?), write the "Sword" on a plate of copper (kyprinon) and put it in . . and they will be broken. -- 6. To subdue a woman, write with the blood of thy hand thy (?) name upon thy gate, and write thy name upon a scroll of leather of a hart with the blood of thy finger, and say this "Sword," and she will come to thee.

-- 7. To make thyself praised in the community, take in thy left hand porret-seed and utter over it the "Sword," and throw it between them,3 and descend (?) until the sun sets, and he will carry thee wherever thou wishest, and fast for three days, and burn incense and the smoke of white flower, and repeat the "Sword" in the morning and the evening, and he will come instantly and speak to thee and do thy bidding.

-- 8. To get information through a dream, take balm and write upon "Chartis hieratikon," and repeat the "Sword" in front of a light, and put out the light with a stick of olive-wood, and lie down. -- 9. If thou wishest to go to a great man, take rose-oil and repeat the "Sword" over the oil and anoint thy hands and face with it, and he will hearken unto thee. -- 10. To make strife in the community, take the left hand full of mustard, speak the "Sword" over it, and throw it amongst them, and they will kill one another.

-- ll. To separate a man from his wife, take ass's meat in thy hand and say over it the "Sword," and no harm will befall thee (?). -- 12. To destroy thy enemy, take a leaden plate and some of his halr and clothes, and say the "Sword" over them, and bury them in a deserted house, and he will fall down. -- 18. To walk in the street and not to be recognized by anyone, take wormwood, perfumes, and soot, and moke thyself with it, and take the heart of a fox, and say the "Sword," and go out in the street. -- 14. If you are on the sea and the storm rages, stand up against the waves and say the "Sword" to them, and they will go down; then write on a plate, or potsherd, or a piece of wood, and hang it in front of the ship, and it will not founder. -- 15. To break an enemy, write the "Sword" upon a potsherd that has not yet hem burned, and plaster it over, and throw it into his house. -- 16. To obtain anything thou likest, take into thy right hand wormwood, and say over it the "Sword" facing the sun, and everything will be fulfilled, and purify thyself for seven days, and thou wilt prosper in everything. Do kind deeds to thy friends, take heed not to take an oath, and walk modestly, and thus thou wilt prosper.

Write X upon the palm of thy left hand, take then a new lamp and fill it with olive-oil and naphtha, and put on new clean clothes, and sleep in a clean house, and the angel will come at once and wake thee,, and reveal unto thee everything that thou wishest.

III. R. Akiba asked R. Eliezer the great: "How can one make the Angel of the Presence descend upon earth to reveal to man the mysteries from above and beneath, and the speculations of the foundations of heavenly and earthly things, and the treasures of wisdom, cunning, and help?" He said thereupon to me: "My son! I once made him come down, and he nearly destroyed the whole world, for he is a mighty prince and greater than any in the heavenly cohort, and he ministers oontinually before the King of the Universe, with purity and separation, and with fear and dread of the glory of his Master, because the Shekinah is always with him." And he said to him: "My master, by the glory which thou hast bestowed upon me, I conjure thee to instruct me how to attach him to me." (And he replied) : "In that hour when I wish to attach him to me and to employ him, I sit and fast on that very day ; but prior to it one must keep oneself free for seven days from any nocturnal impurity, and must bathe in the fountain of water, and not speak at all during those seven days, and at the end of this purification, on the day of the fast, he must sit in the water up to his throat, and before he utters the conjuration he must first say: 'I conjure you, angels of dread, fear, and shaking, who are appointed to hurt those who are not pure and clean and desire the services of my heavenly servants -- I conjure you in the name of X, who is mighty over all, and rules over all, and everything is in His hands, that you do not hurt me, nor terrify me, nor frighten me; verily, in the name of the powerful, the head of . . .' After this he may commence his conjuration, for now he has fortified himself and has sealed himself with the name of God of 42 letters, before which all who hear it tremble and are frightened, and the heavenly hosts are terror-struck. He must then again conjure, and say: 'X, chief, who of all the destroying angels is the most hurtful and burning, with this Name and in this way I call thee AVZHIA, angel of the Presence, youthful minister before the King of the Universe, who art a prince and chief of the heavenly hosts; I conjure thee and decree upon thee that thou attachest thyself to me to fulfil my wish and to accept the decree of my conjuration and to accomplish my desires and fulfil my wishes, and do not frighten me, nor terrify me, nor overawe me, and do not make my frame shake and my feet vacillate, nor cause my speech to be perverted; but may I be fortified and strengthened, and may the conjuration be effective and the (sacred) Name uttered properly by my throat, and may no vacillation take hold of me and no trembling of the feet by thy ministering angels confuse me and overawe me, and weaken my hands, and may I not be overcome by the fire and flame of the storm and whirlwind which precedes thee, O wonderful and exalted one, whose Ineffable name is X, of whose wrath the earth trembles, and nothing can withstand his anger, twice blessed. Again I conjure thee by thy 14 (!) names by which thou didst reveal thyself to thy prophets and seers, to place in their mouths sweet words of prophecy and to utter pleasant words; and these are the Ineffable names and their surnames (Kunya): Spirit Piskonnit, kunya, X; Atimon, kunya, X; Piskon (?), Hugron, kunya, X; Sanigron, kunya, X; Msi, kunya, X; Mokon, kunya, X; Astm, kunya, X; Sktm, kunya, X; Ihoaiel, kunya, X; lofiel, kunya, X; Ssnialiah, kunya, X; Kngieliah, kunya, X; Zabdiel, kunya, X. I conjure thee with these fourteen names, by which all the secrets and mysteries and signs are sealed and accomplished, and which are the foundations of heaven and earth. Four of these are engraved upon the heads of the Hayoth (Holy Greaturee), namely -- X, the lord of powers; X, master of miracles; X, master of purity; and X master of the yoke. And four are engraved upon the four sides of the Throne, namely -- X, three times holy; X, Adir, Adiri, Adiron, etc., the king of kings. And four are engraved upon the four crowns of the Ofanim (wheels) that stand against the Holy Creatures, as it is said: "When those went, these went; and when those stood, these stood" (Ezek. i, 21); and these they are -- X, who is the mightiest over all; X, who rules over all the inhabitants of the heights (?), and in whese hands everything is. And two are engraved upon the crown of the most exalted and high King, and these they are -- X, before whom every knee bends and every mouth utters praises; X, besides him there is no God and helper. With these names I conjure thee, and firmly decree upon thee to descend quickly to me, N, son of N, thou and not thy messenger. And when thou comest down do not turn my mind, but reveal unto me all the secret mysteries from above and beneath, and the hidden secrets from above and beneath, and all the secrets of wisdom and the cunning of helpfulness, just as a man speaks to his neighbour. For I have conjured thee with these Names, that are great and mighty and wonderful and awe-inspiring, and proved and arranged in proper order, through which the glorious throne has been established and the beautiful seat of the Most High, which has been wonderfully wrought, long before thou and the heavenly hosts had been created, "While as yet He had not made the earth nor the fields, and the inhabitants of the earth and the creatures therein" (Prov. viii, 26).

"'I call thee further by (the power) of the five selected Names, to which only one is superior, and this is their form -- X. I conjure thee by these five Names, which correspond to the five names of God, whose letters are written on burning fire, and they circle round the throne of glory, one ascending and the other descending, so that the angels of the Presence should not behold them, and this is their equivalent and form and glory -- X. I conjure thee by these, as thou knowest their praise and greatness, which no mouth can utter, and no ear can hear, no, not even one of them. Thou hast been commanded and ordered by the Most High: "as soon as thou hearest anyone conjuring thee with these names, to do honour to My Name, and to descend quickly and fulfil the wish of the man who makes thee hear them; but if thou tarriest I will push thee into the fiery river Rigayon and place another in thy stead." Do it, therefore, for His Name, and come quickly to me, N, son of N, not in a terror, and not in fear, not with fiery coals, not with hailstone, and not with the sleet and treasures of snow, and not with the howling of the storm, and not with the provinces of the whirlwind that usually accompany thee, and do my bidding and fulfil my desire, for everything is in thy hand; by the permission of thy God, the master over all and thy lord, and with His Names I conjure thee to attach thyself quickly to me; come and fulfil my wish, and do not tarry.

"'I further call thee with the greatest of thy Names, the pleasant and beloved one, which is the same as that of thy Master, save one letter, with which He created and formed everything, and which He placed as a seal upon all the work of His hand; and this is its equivalent -- X, and the other in the language of purity (permutations of the letters Yod, He) is read so -- X. I conjure thee with the right hand of sanctity and with His beloved Name, in whose honour everything has been created, and all are terror-struck by His mighty arm, and all the sons of the internal heavenly cohort (servants) tremble and shake of Him fear, which is X, and its equivalent by means of JHVH is X. Blessed be the name of His glorious kingdom for ever and ever. And all praise and extol thy Name, for they love thee. I conjure thee, and decree upon thee firmly, not to disobey my words, and not to alter my decree and my decision with which I conjured thee, and decreed upon thee, and established in peace. In the Name X, blessed be the name of His glorious kingdom for ever and ever, depart in peace, and do not frighten me in the hour of thy departure; in the name X, Lord, most high and holy, in the name of the Lord of Hosts, the God of Israel's battalions; in the name of the holy living Creatures, and in the name of the Wheels of the Chariot, and in the name of the river of fire, Ih, Zii, Ziin, and all His ministers, and in the name of IH, Ziin, Sabaoth, Z, El Z, Shaddai Z, X revealed Himself on Mount Sinai in the glory of His majesty.

"'With these Names, terrible and mighy, which darken the sun, and obscure the moon, and turn the sea, and break the rocks, and extinguish the light, I conjure you, spirits, and . . and Shiddim, and Satanim, that yen depart and disappear from N, son of N.'"

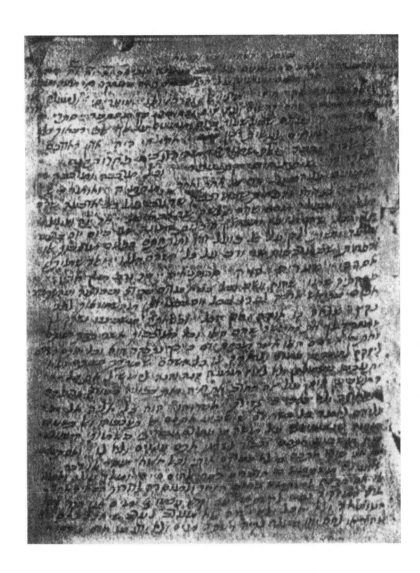

APPENDIX II.

I. Against an enemy. -- I call thee, evil spirit, cruel spirit, merciless spirit. I call thee, bad spirit, who sittest in the cemetery and takes away healing from man. Go and place a knot in NN's head, in him eyes, in his mouth, in his tongue, in his throat, in his windpipe; put poisonous water in his belly. If you do not go and put water in his belly, I will send against you the evil angels Puziel, Guziel, Psdiel, Prziel. I call thee and those six knots that you go quickly to NN and put poisonous water in his belly and kill NN whom I mean (or, because I wish it). Amen, Amen. Selah.

II. Against an enemy. -- Write upon a new-laid egg on a Nazarene cemetery: "I conjure you, luminaries of heaven and earth, as the heavens are separated from the earth, so separate and divide NN from him wife NN, and separate them from one another, as life is separated from death, and sea from dry land, and water from fire, and mountain from vale, and night from day, and light from darkness, and the sun from the moon; thus separate NN from NN his wife, and separate them from one another in the name of the twelve hours of the day and the three watches (?) of the night, and the seven days of the week, and the thirty days of the month, and the seven years of Shemittah, and the fifty years of Jubilee, on every day, in the name of the evil angel Tmsmael, and in the name of the angel Iabiel, and in the name of the angel Drsmiel, and in the name of the angel Zahbuk, and in the name of the angel Ataf, and in the name of the angel Zhsmael, and in the name of the angel Zsniel, who preside over pains, sharp pains, inflammation, and dropsy, and separate NN from him wife NN, make them depart from one another, and that they should not comfort one another, swiftly and quickly."

Made in the USA
Columbia, SC
05 March 2021